Cairn

Cairn
Richie McCaffery

ISBN: 978-0-9927589-1-2

First published June 2014 by:

Nine Arches Press
PO Box 6269
Rugby
CV21 9NL
United Kingdom

www.ninearchespress.com

Printed in Britain by:

imprintdigital.net
Seychelles Farm,
Upton Pyne,
Exeter
EX5 5HY
United Kingdom
www.imprintdigital.net

Cairn

Richie McCaffery

Nine
Arches
Press

new poets series

CONTENTS

Nothing corrects
the haircracks in the crockery.

– **Alan Riach**

DEDICATION

In an underground copy
of *Lady Chatterley's Lover*
a shaky plum inscription:

'To Renee, my sweet –
from France via the Dunkirk
holocaust, 2/8/40, Sid'

All that way in a kitbag,
through panzers and snipers.
Bullets hitting the water
like kingfishers.

BALLAST FLINT

They often took people from these shores,
pariahs of the law or kirk. Sent them down
into the holds of ships like ballast flint,
mined locally, as plentiful useless weight.

Nodules like bone joints, broken open
to dark quartz, the black iris of a Sphinx,
unknowable and inscrutable. The dud cargo
often dumped by the salt-chapped rim

of other seas where it did not belong,
still cluttering beaches. It once sparked
great fires, sharpened to double-edged blade,
a forgotten clan knapping arms in the swash.

SCHOOL

That boy who played the flute
much better than you ever could
died a few years ago by his own hand.

The seed your daughter planted
is now a tree they're going to fell;
it undermines the road.

A ball dribbled by the wind
in the playground after the bell rang
turned out to be the globe.

LATE RED ADMIRAL

It came in with the last of the logs,
a shrivelled pod of staircase wit.

After a few days of inglenook glow,
the butterfly hatched in a winter pub,

an applause of wings, out of time
with the rest of the world's good deeds.

WALLET

While clearing out the old bureau we find it,
his sun-tanned wallet from the Africa Campaign.
Goatskin fobbed off as camel-hide in a souk,
the first time he had paper money to squander.

It is autumn about the house where he wintered,
bronchial scratches of branches lay down leaves
like the wind is a briber with his wad of notes;
something is buying itself back into bud.

Last Lot of the Day

A mother-of-pearl inlaid, walnut-veneered
writing slope with a scabby purple velvet
surface for dip-pen, paper and blotter.

Inside a secret compartment, a sheet of mint
Penny Reds, a bundle of blank envelopes
with black edges as if mourning has no-one

particular in mind, and no clear address.
You might think of the dead that never died
to leave this surplus, as if they were saved.

ST. LAWRENCE'S

Sunday, the organ is lowing
like the last harpooned whale.

People take its blubber to light
lamps inside themselves.

Something has died in great pain,
I am not the one to say what.

The doors open, light floods in,
and suddenly we are drowning.

PRESS

When times got really bad
you tightened the screws

on your childhood flower press
squeezing one last time.

We never saw the blossoms
laid to rest in tissue paper.

I dreamt I opened it to find
the garden flowering in darkness.

ALBUM

For Douglas Dunn

After dinner he showed me
his stamp albums, the spoils
of a life-time of collecting.

Fine rows of neat specimens,
tiny hack-saw edges,
priced in spent currencies.

Regimes had been toppled,
stamps smuggling out news.
Though the cursive letters

were long discarded,
the senders and recipients
reached the same address.

POLICE WHISTLE

In a drawer of his old ties
I find it, squat and silver,
my Grandfather's whistle.

I blow it so loud and urgent
that even he hears in the dark
of his keyless oubliette.

And with a great swooping
of mahogany truncheons
and gas lamps across dark moors,

a breaking of wax seals,
and questing of blood hounds,
all the unsolved crimes

of a hundred years are answered
and justice is meted out
on the eardrums of passers-by.

THE CONSUL

You are unhappy here, in Paris,
in your birthplace, everywhere.

If you were a God tasked with
ripping open two tectonic plates

to put a new island on the map
in basalt spuming out of the sea,

you couldn't begin to populate it
with all the dead people you miss.

But as a start, tell me the weed
you want for a national flower.

I'll pin it to my lapel, like a consul
to a place that is still to exist.

Spoon

A deserter from a service, left pearl black
after years of clammy hands.

Once polished it revealed a tiny gilded bowl,
a Midas trick which pleased you, but jarred me.

The thought of which truth someone was forced
to swallow, to need so fine a spoon as that.

BOOKMARK

Left as a marker in a boring book,
a yellowed flyer for *The Gondoliers.*
Put on by the amateur players
at the Theatre Royal in the 40s

where my Grandmother sang
and Grandfather sat, watching.
I leave it like an alternate page,
a shortcut straight to the end.

ASH

There is as much ash
in a smoked tab as there is
in a cremated finger.

The finger in question
was nicotine-stained
and prone to point and jab.

God had a good long drag
on that one. Stubbed
it out in a rented ossuary.

SALVAGE

Pushing sixty,
my mother still plays the orphan
as we pass a skip
on our way back from a pub.

She fishes out
old broken Art Nouveau tiles
of faience flowers
from a smashed hearth.

Once home
she pieces together
the heart
of a fallen household.

THE TRUTH SO FAR

In the chalky trough under the blackboard,
lessons dusted and already forgotten.

The teacher is squawking away once more,
scratching into the tabula rasa

the truths about God and arithmetic
with the expungeable white of fossil shells.

HOMECOMING

for Edwin Morgan

By the time I got home from a cul-de-sac job,
the makar had been cremated in Glasgow.

That evening, poet-friends boasted sightings of him,
Canedolian rara avis, most lyrical starling.

I have a memory of sipping tea at Clarence Court
and the afternoon sun the brightest I'd seen.

As we talked of Veronica Forrest-Thomson
I felt my dead grandfather growing jealous.

The sun seethed when Eddie spoke, the light
of a mothership glaring between high tenements.

STEP-FATHER

He's like that sad town you took us to
when you found your blood family.
A place of abandoned colliery terraces,
their roofs slowly caving in to beams
holding dirty huddling pigeons,
their petrol-slick plumage
mimicking the shades of lost slates.

Similar in certain lights, but different,
his face as pink as our father's was,
every bit the man he was, so you say.
But for every parallel you pin on him
I see pigeons for slates, and rain coming.

Saint Bavo

A cathedral as ornate as a geode
the size of fifty quarries.

On the floor we found
a tiny cartouche

of a white heart, laid centuries
back and forgotten,

our vision whittled down
to the smallest labour of love,

bruised by dirty soles,
and grounded in this vastness.

Black Sheep Inn

Sometimes this guilt I cart around
is lead-flashing stolen from a clock spire.

Now there's a Swiss-made metal scarab
on my wrist rubbing grains in its hands.

I have amassed regret like pearling grit
in the belly of a freshwater mussel.

I can bend myself to any drunkard's ear,
dream of a golden sentence to set me free.

7 PUDDEN WYND

When they built the house back in 1892,
someone put a dated stone escutcheon
upside down above the door.

I pass it every day and wonder
what it's like to live in a house
where time stands on its head.

Behind mouldering bay windows
strange things happen daily,
broken vases repairing themselves,

a place where the dead are anything but.
In the kitchen they un-bake stale bread.
Nothing is ever lost at this spider-eyed address

and I can't decide, from the outside
whether it's a blessing or curse to never
be able to lose something, or someone.

OLD SCHOOL

Though the doctor wrote with a gold-nibbed pen,
he did little to gild my father's leaden news.

Even as willow boughs drooped on the garden
your mother would not yield this time.

In town I saw a young man with an old school tie
like a rope he'll always use to haul himself aboard.

NEGATIVES

A suitcase full, sheets
of gelatine, clotting
to bleary half-memory.

The celluloid too far gone
to be developed,
you hold each one
to a bay window,

seeing light where
there was darkness
and lunar-silver dark
in the place of light.

The x-rays they showed us
of his lungs,
dotted maps to no-where.

NOUGHTS AND CROSSES

The other evening with nothing much to do
I played noughts and crosses within panes
of my sash window. I pretended you
joined in from the other side of the world
and I tried my best not to let you win.

We played with bits of scrap paper
I'd tacked over the glass and felt-tipped,
not stopping until a pattern emerged,
your clean winning troika of crosses
and my scattering of zeros.

At last the view from my window was gone
leaving only the clarity of your strategies
and the doodling clutter of indecision
that has brought and kept me here.

Miss Anderson's pen

I write with an old *Parker 51*
which was Miss Anderson's.
I know this because her name
is engraved into its silver cap.

I never knew Miss Anderson,
yet I use her pen to scrawl
terrible slanders, obscenities
and secrets she never knew.

Miss Anderson sounds like she
might've been a schoolteacher,
I'm a lazy student of literature –
the nib must be so confused.

I imagine Miss Anderson read
absence letters from parents
who wrote with similar pens.
She'd blot the register with hers.

I wonder if she had children,
and wrote them letters of illness
the way I'm writing this down
in Miss Anderson's absence.

BROTHER

I survived dinner on only one bottle
of burgundy. You could have dived
to the wreck on a lung full of air.

You wore suits like a mountain wears trees.
I wear finer cuts no better than the hanger.
Today I am grief clad in obsidian wools.

Your shelf groans with dusty trophies;
you beat me in every sports-day race
and kept running for no award.

Rust

In the dunes at Warkworth beach,
wartime barbed wire corrodes
in marram grass, coiled like cilices.

All the gins in the Duke's woods
lie shut in leaf pulp, their teeth
stuck in a lockjaw of oxidation.

The languages I used to speak,
that ferric tang when you cough,
the staples in booklets that failed us.

THE WEIGHT

You asked me to move the big bag of compost
from the bottom garden to your flowerbed.

It had been raining all day the day before
and the bag was heavy, too heavy to carry.

I think of him sometimes, as you probably do,
lying in his little plot of earth and how

the days when it rains always seem to be
the days when he lies heavy in the mind.

COLD CALLER

Nearly all the names and numbers
in her leatherette phone book
are crossed or scribbled out.

One of these days I'll dial
a dead number, wait and listen.

There will come a voice
cracked as a dry clarinet reed.

They remember me as a boy
and ask how school's going.

When I tell them I'm now a man
they twig and hang up
on my cruel prank.

The Rapture

Yesterday was Judgment Day.
We were stuck on an inter-city bus
in a traffic jam like a fleet of clippers
threaded through the neck of a Codd's bottle,
an exodus on a single-lane road.

Somewhere in God's granite allotment plots,
nanotechnologies of hatred and grudges
were stirring the blessed restful soil,
the dead limbering up for a carious dash
to the hot seat, stray dogs salivating.

Cars dropped in ditches like windowsill flies.
A petrol tanker was the first to run out of fuel.
The wind turned punk, a man began to cry,
stuck for hours, a busload bound for eternity
unable to stand each other for a sweaty evening.

Only those with a destination will be lost.
You woke and spoke of maybe next year
for your baby, coming off the pills for good.
My watch hit six and the light was snatched away;
raindrops danced like sperm on the window.

Elizabeth Logan (1837 - 1839)

Her small stone is gadrooned like a prototype
for the postage stamp, in a field of dead letters
addressed to God.

It quietly states its limestone obituary, the last
example of Hugh Miller's rupestrine writing.

So steady was the hand that chiselled this
copperplate, the same hand that with hammer
wrought in strata to discover
the *Terra incognita of wonders.*

In the course of a single tide he had found
a shoal of fossil fish, breaking them open
to the light as an unseen riptide of fever
swept his daughter away.

BOTTLE-DIGGING

Now we value this land for building
that was once only fit for bottle-dumps,
so the steel mitt of a digger, like a waiter
brings up hundreds of Victorian bottles;
Codd's, Hamilton's and Hutchinson's.

We value what was discarded;
fragile vials of century old hangovers,
they spill out from a broken hill,
the dead realising they are dead,
drinking the wakes of even the living.

ARRIVAL

When my mother arrived,
no one would sign for her,
left out like a parcel
on a stranger's doorstep.

Bundle of birth, fly-tipped,
swathed in a linen bag
stamped *Tate and Lyle sugar*
seven pounds too heavy.

No mobile, just rain clouds,
her lips sapphire blue,
tiny lungs like strawberries
full of pneumonia.

INK

My father keeps bringing back
bottles of vintage ink
from car boot sales
like *Stephens' Radiant Blue*

He knows I like fountain pens
and offers me not wisdom
nor advice, but the blueberry
wine of unwritten words.

He hasn't always been there
for me, but he knows that,
so he transfuses my pen
with something he's bottled up.

THE PROFESSIONAL

You ask what I do for a living
and I don't think I can say.
There is something in the way
I take this teacup from you
without the tell-tale click
of ring on hot porcelain.

You ask, *Will this take long?*
Maybe. My questions must
be answered. Some are pointless
as wasps and the pain they give.
Others will take you many lungs
to satisfy the depth required.

Remember my dolphin smile,
my signature like snake-crossed sand.
You will notice some day soon
all your cups carry my trademark –
a faint hairline crack. I specialise
in subtle, half-bearable damage.

PLIMSOLLS

My mother took a permanent marker
to write my name on the inner sole,
so every step I took told the world I was here
and I belonged to her and a clan before me.

Now I wear boots with another name
like so many others do. The spoors
I left in text books, carved in desks
with a compass are long erased.
What remains is what she said:
You're your own man, boy.

BUTTONS

Predictable truth-or-dare question –
Have you ever stolen anything?
I filled my little pockets

with buttons from craft at school –
Victorian jet, mother-of-pearl
and old bone fasteners.

The remains of vanished garments
from a famously buttoned-up age.
The past undressing itself,

ripping off its voluminous bodice
to reveal a village of dead folk
reduced to a jar of old studs.

SEASIDE HOTEL

There's always another flute
of shipwreck champagne
to tickle the throat,

by evening, I hear folkloric blethers
of those who got beyond the dirty sands
and the dark headland

to find coves with crumbling hotels
like stranded clippers
widowed by the sea.

SAMPLER

Foxed and moth-nicked, dated 1892,
made by a girl of ten to prove in stitches
she knew her numbers, the alphabet
and an anodyne quatrain from the Bible.

She gave up counting until she was found
in place of her words, silk cursive letters.
Where she pricked her finger, droplets
that darkened into whorls of rust.

EDELWEISS

Every year in the cloudy altitudes of Thyon,
he searched for a sprig of his 'ugly flower',
as if looking for the moly that would save him.

There were years of rages, scorched earth
between us. It is only now I look back on this folly
and see how rare and strenuous his love could be.

In Praise of Sash Windows

Best of all the old sash windows,
every bubble and dimple a reminder
the glassblower once drew breath.

Flaking, blunt wooden guillotines
where hundreds of summer winds
have been carefully beheaded.

Behind the bleary panes, weights
of lead hanging, boxed into the wall
and unseen by anyone alive.

TESSERAE

She told me how she lost her first,
the ordeal in a tiled avocado bathroom,

I thought of all the lost Roman mosaics,
tiny tesserae of vitreous gods

wearing pottery garlands of dead corn,
under the rapeseed of Northumberland,

floorscapes of the great abandoned villas
hidden in soil too fertile for burial.

Moon

By the time the scrap-men took my Dad's car
he had travelled the equivalent of a return
journey to the moon, by only driving to work.

All those spring-heeled astronauts
with their bumper-sticker Stars & Stripes
bringing back samples of lunar dirt.

Dad voyaged just as far, less in space than time
discovering nothing but dirty cuffs, each trip
leaving behind a cairn, in pieces of himself.

X

The lawnmower's drone is almost a small,
rescue plane. To the dead, both are far overhead.

The other day in a local antique shop we found
an old compass with a fifth airt carved onto it.

We could follow that direction for all our years
and end up back in the same place.

The mower-man goes over graves, and lays
snapped stone crosses flat on tended earth.

IVORIES

for Theo Hedley's first birthday

He is as old as one new ring,
another inch in a tree trunk's waist.
Tonight Theo is teething, and sleep
is the downy stuff of dreams.
In the bloodshot morning, an ingot
of pure white is set in his pink gums.

The sun is a slow hydrogen bomb
detonating in the permafrosts of Alaska.
Netsukes of shattered Mammoth tusk
collect in zones of ablation. Ivories
appearing from the unknown, Theo
cutting his teeth on the bones in a cave.

THE LONESOME DEATH OF BRIAN CONNOLLY

His last great gig
was falling backwards
down the stairs, pissed,
as if letting go into
the needy arms of the crowd,
his heart rattling
like the Glasgow Subway shuttle
between Hillhead and Kelvinbridge,
riding twenty years
with the same expired ticket.

Viv

For years my Grandma's best friend Viv
has been referred to as *The lady who got run over,*

and what smarts to this day is the question
where she was heading, across that main road.

She was in the middle of nowhere,
a little gabardine matador. I often think

Grandma might sleep easier if she knew
Viv had a destination, beyond the crossing.

GIL MARTIN

Growing up, most of my clothes
were at the very least second hand.
Some of the shirts and jackets
still carried old owner's names
sewn into the scruff of the neck.

I'd go to school in George's best shirt,
in winter wear Robert's cenotaph coat.
As a teenager, I'd leave dirty clothes
strewn, as if there'd been a wild orgy
of a party somewhere in the near past,

where the owners of the clothes
had been so drunk they'd forgotten
all about themselves, even their names.
I remained the host, but was dressed
as all of my dearly departed guests.

PEVSNER GUIDES

He had the full set for every county
and thought humans a blot on holiday snaps.

He would never go without the right guide
but he's away now and the bookshelf has no gaps.

In every photo there is no sign of him, bar
the spectral smear, a huge finger in the sky.

TIES

As a policeman,
my Granddad's ties
were clip-on

coming away easy
like a salamander tail
if someone throttled him.

He died, suffocated
in an open necked shirt,
the victim of his tobacco habit.

I borrowed a black tie
from my father
to attend his funeral.

Dad has many black ties.
I thank him for the Windsor knot
which I slacken or tighten

like the grip between
his hand
and his father's.

WARKWORTH

Some locals still remember the errand boy
shot from his bike passing the hotel
while inside a sergeant cleaned his pistol.

Tonight I walk past a different window
and think of your eyes behind the pane
taking aim with only an accidental glance.

BARNEY

collected postcards, old ones,
particularly from places bombed
or bulldozed, where street names
were just the hearsay of ghosts,
their stamps colourful shibboleths.

He'd vanish for days with no word
in search of those lost addresses.
Nowadays we wait for postcards
he sends second-class from the night
that always say *Wish you were here.*

SPINNING PLATES

My mother was mad as mercury,
mad as a silken Disraeli stovepipe
hat hiding a gypsum-white rabbit.

She once told me – the malt talking –
I wasn't her first born boy;
there had been seminal drafts.

She said being pregnant
was like spinning a bone-china plate
on the thinnest stick inside you –

breakages were bound to occur.
It was a question of which piece
could drop intact and roll around

on a hardwood floor, its rim ringing
with cries. My sister is wild firing,
an artisan's multi-coloured plate

still atwirl. I am a white canteen
saucer, ready to be tanned with tea-
slops. A cupped palm for spillage.

THE LEAN-TO

I only noticed the lean-to was there
after a storm had brought it down.

It left behind an un-weathered space
on the north flank of the big house.

I saw then both structures had relied
on the other for support or protection,

how years together made them one
and that absence has its own presence.

SIGHTING

After Derick Thomson

As children we often went hunting
for ghosts, armed with rock-pool nets
to nip at their wispy joss-stick trains.

We never found one, they were always
one life-time ahead, dropping dead leaves,
vanishing as we came round the bend.

I am looking for the ghost of a boy,
a man hunting for a haunting
that happened here many years ago.

ACKNOWLEDGEMENTS

Thanks are due to the editors of the following magazines, e-zines, anthologies and pamphlets in which some of these poems first appeared:

Magazines:

Agenda; The Dark Horse; The Delinquent; Drey; Envoi; Fire; Gutter; HQ Quarterly; The Interpreter's House; Iota; Magma; The Manhattan Review; New Walk; The North; Orbis; The Reader; The Rialto; The SHOp; Smiths Knoll; Southlight; Stand; Under the Radar; Valve; The Warwick Review.

E-zines:

3:AM; And Other Poems; B O D Y; From Glasgow to Saturn; The Harlequin; The Irish Literary Review; The Lampeter Review; The Manchester Review; The Prague Revue; Snakeskin; Stride.

Anthologies:

Best British Poetry 2012; Best Scottish Poems 2012.

Pamphlets:

Spinning Plates – Happen*Stance* Press, 2012
Ballast Flint – Cromarty Arts Trust, 2013